# Ballet

# Ballet

ROBINA BECKLES WILLSON

HAMLYN
LONDON · NEW YORK · SYDNEY · TORONTO

Published 1982 by
The Hamlyn Publishing Group Limited
London · New York · Sydney · Toronto
Astronaut House, Feltham, Middlesex, England

ISBN 0 600 31600 9

Printed in Italy

Previous page: *The Dutch National Ballet in* Moments.

## Acknowledgements

All the photographs in this book are by Jesse Davis, Mike
Davis Studio Ltd., with the exception of the following:

Ballet Rambert–Alan Cunliffe 37, 41; BBC, London 76;
Zoe Dominic, London 80 right; Photographie Giraudon,
Paris 45 left, 72 right; Hamlyn Group Picture Library 28
inset, 33, 45 right, 74–75, 77, 98; The Raymond Mander
and Joe Mitcheson, London 72 left; Mansell Collection,
London 28, 46 left, 50, 51, 54 top, 54 bottom, 56, 57, 57
inset; Musée des Beaux Arts, Nantes 46 right; National
Film Archive, London 39, 91; Royal Ballet–Leslie E. Spatt
65 right; Victoria and Albert Museum, London 26–27, 38
right, 49, 52, 60 top left, 60 bottom; Reg Wilson, London
17 bottom.

Illustrations by Oriol Bath

# Contents

# Introduction

This pocket book is a first guide to a world which is increasingly full of variety. There is so much to know about ballet and to enjoy. There are the dancers and teachers and many other people who work together to make ballet. Dancing has now been brought within reach of enormous new audiences worldwide. You can join them. At home, television programmes can show you exactly how a dancer is trained, what happens in a class, how older dancers sometimes teach roles, originally created for them, to new dancers.

The earlier history of ballet still lives on in its dancers. When Anton Dolin (born in 1904), acted the part of the famous ballet teacher, Enrico Cecchetti (born in 1850), in the recent film, *Nijinsky*, he owned and used the original stick with which Cecchetti used to point and tap at dancers' feet.

Ballet's history, to which this book introduces you, can be seen in the old classical ballets, which are still regularly performed today. They are large spectacles, with magnificent scenery and big casts in beautiful costumes. *The Sleeping Beauty* is a good example of one of these spectacles.

All through the history of ballet, different people have tried new ways of telling a story or saying something in dance. There are modern versions of old classics too. For example, on film you can see Rudolf Nureyev and Margot Fonteyn in *Romeo*

*Rudolf Nureyev and Patricia Ruanne in a production of* The Sleeping Beauty *for the* Nureyev festival. Nureyev *has brought new life to classical ballet.*

*and Juliet.* Kenneth MacMillan did the choreography, which means he worked out all the steps. As a choreographer and director Nureyev has created his own version using the same music by Prokofiev, and again dancing Romeo himself. Finding your way through the ballet world, you will see that even with the same choreography, each performance varies. You can collect your old programmes and compare different performances and productions.

You will find it very exciting going to a live performance when the dancers re-create the ballet for you, bringing its story to life. This needs great artistry, because the dancers will have been through each movement countless times in hours of rehearsals and other performances, and then have to present the result of all the hard work again to

Left: *Monica Mason rehearsing with the choreographer. The picture shows her intense concentration on what she is doing.*

Below: *A dancer at the Royal Opera House, London. She looks excited and happy in a splendid costume. The picture shows the cast dressed up and ready to perform.*

you, their new audience. The ballet must never look weary or stale, as if the dancers are bored with their parts. There will always be somebody in a large audience, watching even the most unimportant member of the *corps de ballet*, the supporting dancers. Each one must dance as if she were the ballerina in the spotlight. This is achieved partly by hard training (having to dance, whether she feels well or ill, fresh or tired), and partly by responding to an audience. A good performing dancer enjoys giving pleasure to the audience, by conveying the choreographer's intentions properly, and by doing credit to the preparation and guidance of the director, who has moulded the dancers into a united cast.

The performers need the qualities of dancers, actors and athletes to do all that eager audiences expect of them. Nowadays ballet is often more than just telling a story in dance. Modern dance has changed the idea of ballet. To make audiences more knowledgeable as well as enthusiastic, some modern groups and companies have left their theatres and gone out to attract and build up audience support. They have split up and visited schools and colleges, to show open rehearsals, choreography being worked out, and to demonstrate training for modern dance. Directors of modern companies want their audiences to feel that dance improves their lives, because it can express feelings and moods, and the audience can share by watching or even by taking up modern dance themselves.

*The London Festival Ballet dancing in* The Three-Cornered Hat. *The ballet is based on Spanish dances, performed to music by Manuel de Falla.*

Robert Cohan, an American working in Britain, has choreographed a work called *Waterless Method of Swimming Instruction*, which includes amusing actions in a set representing the empty swimming pool of an ocean liner. His idea started, when he read a swimming manual in which young boys practised swimming 'dry', balancing on benches. He turned this idea into a ballet in which dancers mime the movements of swimming and diving while dancing. Sometimes they shuffle round with their ankles in lifebelts, or teasingly imprison a dancer in a high pile of rubber rings. Another dancer, as a sunbather, deals with an awkward deckchair, walking and posing, but not actually dancing at all.

So, a ballet can be dancing or some new experiments of modern dance companies. In this book, you can find out how ballet began, and who shaped its development. You can learn how dancers become professional, and how all of them have to start with first classes, and struggle, in the beginning, to control their feet, legs, arms, head and body all at once.

If everything about ballet was taken to pieces, it would spoil the magic. But you can begin to realize the delight in dancing, with this book as your introduction.

Right: *Great care is taken to make sure that costumes fit properly. They must be comfortable and stand up to strenuous performances.*

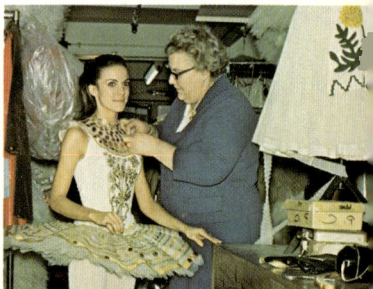

Below: *A scene from the Royal Ballet's* Punch and the Street Party, *choreographed by David Bintley.*

# Famous ballets

There are so many ballets to enjoy, that you will have to watch some of all the different periods and styles, and see various dancers interpreting them, before you will find your favourites. Each production will be different. Dancers will portray characters and work out parts in their own ways. Look out for these ballets. You may be able to see them live, in cinemas or on television.

### *La Fille Mal Gardée, Vain Precautions* or *The Unchaperoned Daughter* (1786)

This ballet was first performed in Bordeaux, France, to a collection of French popular songs and airs. It was one of the first ballets to deal with everyday life, and had many revivals and new

productions during the 19th century. The version you can see today is Frederick Ashton's own production for the Royal Ballet, in 1960, with music arranged by John Lanchbery.

The story is of a country girl, Lise, who is in love with a young farmer, Colas. Lise's mother wants her to marry another young man, just because he is the wealthy son of a landowner. Yet, however hard she tries, she cannot prevent Lise and Colas from meeting, and finally, she gives way to their wishes.

The ballet is particularly enjoyable, because it is often funny. There is a dance by the cock with all his hens. Lise's mother is danced by a man, just like a pantomime dame, and the highlight of his performance is a superb clog dance.

Opposite: *Nerina Blair as Lise in a country dance in a scene from* La Fille Mal Gardée.

Above: *The famous clog dance from* La Fille Mal Gardée, *with Frederick Ashton as Lise's mother.*

## La Sylphide (1832)

This old ballet has often been revived. August Bournonville, a Danish dancer and choreographer, made his version in 1836, which has been danced by the Royal Danish Ballet ever since, and all over the world. The music is by Jean Schneitzhoeffer.

Filippo Taglioni, the father of the famous dancer Marie Taglioni, was the original choreographer, creating a part for his daughter, which made her famous, and launched a new style. This was the first romantic ballet, and was set in Scotland.

It is the story of James. He is about to marry Effie, but becomes haunted by a beautiful Sylph or Spirit. He leaves Effie and follows the Sylph, but there is no chance of happiness for them because of the witch, Madge. She gives James a magic shawl which she says will help him to capture the Sylph. But, when he wraps it around the Sylph's shoulders, the evil spell begins to work. The Sylph loses her wings and dies. Meanwhile, Effie has married James's rival, Gurn. When James sees the wedding procession, he collapses with grief.

The costume for the Sylph became the uniform for a romantic ballerina. It was a fitting bodice,

with the shoulders bare, little gauze wings, and a bell-shaped muslin skirt falling well below the knees. Dancing on point, on the tips of the toes, made the unearthly Sylph appear to fly.

The Danish dancer and choreographer, Peter Schaufuss, has taken the part of James, and produced *La Sylphide* for the London Festival Ballet and for television in 1980. The sad story still has not lost its appeal for modern audiences.

Left: *A famous partnership between Antoinette Sibley and Anthony Dowell, dancing together in* Giselle.

Opposite top: *A dramatic moment when Giselle is overcome by madness.*

Opposite bottom: *The chorus from a production of* Giselle *by the Bolshoi Ballet.*

## *Giselle* (1841)

This dramatic and romantic ballet has given count-less ballerinas the opportunity to act as well as dance in a demanding part. It has been made into films in America and Russia. The music is by the French composer, Adolphe Adam, the choreo-graphy by two Frenchmen, Coralli and Perrot. It has been popular since its first performance with one of Perrot's pupils, the Italian ballerina Carlotta Grisi, as Giselle.

The story is of a peasant girl, Giselle, who is in love with Albrecht. She thinks that he is a peasant like herself, but he is really a Count, engaged to a Duke's daughter. When Hilarion, a gamekeeper who loves Giselle, jealously tells her that Albrecht is in fact a nobleman, she goes mad and then dies, heartbroken.

In the second act, near Giselle's tomb, the Wilis appear at midnight. They are the spirits of maidens who have died before their weddings, and any man who sees them is forced to dance to his death. Led

by Queen Myrtha, they drive Hilarion into the lake, and attempt to dance Albrecht to his death. But Giselle, now a Wili, saves him by telling him that he will be protected if he holds the cross on her grave. She then dances with him herself until the dawn. Then the Wilis have to return to their graves, and so Albrecht is saved by Giselle's devoted love.

Diaghilev, a Russian ballet producer, took the ballet on tours with his company. Anna Pavlova, a famous Russian dancer, acted the mad Giselle so convincingly in the ballet, that she frightened the other dancers.

## *Coppélia* (1870)

The Emperor of France, Napoleon III, and his Empress Eugénie, attended the first performance of *Coppélia* at the Paris Opéra. With music by the French composer, Delibes, and choreography by Marius Petipa, it was a great success. A later version choreographed by Lev Ivanov and Enrico Cecchetti in Russia in 1894 is the basis for today's popular productions.

Dr Coppélius is a clever toymaker, who can make toys walk and dance, bow and wave. His ambition is to bring one of his clockwork dolls to life by magic. His favourite doll, Coppélia, looks so real, that when he places her on his balcony and winds her up, people passing by wave and smile to her, and she seems to answer them.

When Franz becomes attracted to Coppélia, his girlfriend, Swanhilde, is jealous. So when old Coppélius drops his key in the street, Swanhilde,

Left: *Carole Hill dancing as Coppélia in a London Festival Ballet production. Dr Coppélius is entranced by his favourite doll.*

Opposite: *The ballet ends happily ever after for Franz and Swanhilde. This scene is from a Sadler's Wells Royal Ballet production.*

teased by her jostling young friends, unlocks his door. She and her friends soon discover that the dolls within are clockwork, and they set them in motion. Swanhilde finds Coppélia and, for a joke, puts on her clothes, then hides away when the angry Dr Coppélius returns.

Franz now arrives looking for Coppélia. Coppélius decides to use Franz to try to bring Coppélia to life, and gives him drugged wine and chants spells over him. Swanhilde, dressed in Coppélia's clothes, comes out and dances stiffly for the delighted Doctor. However, she soon turns wildly to destroying his magic book and dolls. Franz awakes

and she forgives him. A village festival ends the ballet. Swanhilde and Franz, and other engaged couples receive purses of gold, and the bewildered Doctor is a little consoled by a present of gold from the Duke.

## *Swan Lake* (1877)

This was one of the first classical ballets to be shown outside Russia. Tchaikovsky's music was not matched by equally good choreography, and the first Moscow performances were not popular. It was successfully revived in St Petersburg (now called Leningrad), with choreography by Petipa and Ivanov, in 1895. Pavlova and Diaghilev both gave shortened versions on their tours abroad. Many later choreographers, such as George Balanchine, have made their own productions.

The story is of Prince Siegfried, who sees the Queen of the Swans, Odette, become a beautiful maiden, when he is out hunting wild swans. She explains that she is under the spell of the wicked magician, Von Rothbart. She is condemned to live as a swan by day, but at night becomes human again. Only when a man swears to love her, and no one else, for ever, will the spell be broken.

Siegfried declares his love, but, at a ball the following evening, he is tricked into asking Odile, the magician's daughter, to marry him. Von Roth-

bart has made her look like Odette, but dressed in black. Choosing Odile from the royal maidens for his bride, Siegfried glances through the window and sees Odette. He realizes his mistake and rushes to find her in the forest, where they are reunited. But the magician says that Siegfried must keep his promise to marry Odile. The only escape is for Siegfried and Odette to die together, so they plunge into the lake, and the spell is broken. The magician dies and Siegfried and Odette find happiness in an after-life.

The twin role of Odette–Odile is danced by one ballerina, who has a marvellous opportunity to dance as the white, loving Odette as well as the black, wicked Odile.

## *The Sleeping Beauty* (1890)

This ballet is based on a fairytale, with music by Tchaikovsky and choreography by Marius Petipa. It is a splendid example of 19th century classical ballet, and it was first presented to the Tsar of Russia.

King Florestan and his queen have invited the Fairies to the christening of their infant daughter, Aurora. Each one dances, waves her wand over the golden cradle and gives a magic present. Before the last one, the Lilac Fairy, can give her gift, she is interrupted by the thunderous arrival of the wicked Fairy, Carabosse, who is furious that she has not been invited to the party.

Carabosse announces that the baby will one day prick her finger on a spindle and die. Everyone is horrified, but the Lilac Fairy still has her present to give. She changes the spell, and says that the princess will not die but, with the whole court, will fall asleep for 100 years, then be woken by a prince's kiss.

At her 16th birthday party, Princess Aurora pricks her finger on a spindle brought by Carabosse in disguise, and, with all the court, falls asleep.

Opposite: *A colourful scene from* The Sleeping Beauty *performed in the Nureyev festival.*

Right and Below: *Patricia Ruanne is Aurora and Rudolf Nureyev the Prince in these scenes.*

After 100 years, Prince Florimund, helped by the Lilac Fairy, makes his way through the enchanted forest and awakens Aurora.

At their wedding, the Fairies dance and celebrate with characters from fairytales, who entertain the guests. Red Riding Hood and the wolf, Puss in Boots and the white cat and beautiful Blue Birds all take their turn.

There are excellent opportunities for solo displays in this ballet, but perhaps the most dazzling dancing is done by the prince and his princess.

### *The Nutcracker* (1892)

Tchaikovsky's music has become so popular that you will probably know his *Nutcracker Suite* before you see the ballet. Petipa wanted to produce the ballet himself but, because of illness, he had to give the job to Ivanov. Petipa's original duet in the ballet for the Sugar Plum Fairy and her partner survives. Other choreographers, Ashton, Balanchine and Nureyev, have made their versions too.

As the ballet opens with a Christmas party it is often performed at Christmas. The cast includes children, some acting as toy soldiers and mice. A little girl, Clara, is given a nutcracker shaped like a toy soldier by Dr Drosselmeyer. Clara's brother, Franz, is jealous, and after a tussle the nutcracker is broken. Franz and Clara are carried off to bed.

Later that night Clara creeps downstairs and finds that the dolls and her nutcracker have come to life bewitched by Dr Drosselmeyer. The Nutcracker and the toy soldiers are attacked by mice, but Clara helps defeat their king by throwing a shoe at him. The Nutcracker becomes a prince, who takes Clara through dancing snowflakes to the Fairy of Ice and Snow. Then they fly to the Kingdom of Sweets, and the Sugar Plum Fairy.

In Clara's honour there is an entertainment. Russian, Arabian, Chinese and Spanish dances are performed, then a gentle Waltz of the Flowers. Clara is overwhelmed by the splendid dances, but becomes sleepy and finds herself back at home. The Christmas tree is no longer brightly lit, and the toys lie on the floor. Clara wonders if it all was a dream.

Above: *An early scene in the Festival Ballet's production of* The Nutcracker.

Below: *A large cast of children enjoying their parts in* The Nutcracker.

Above: *Notice the splendid costumes for the Chinese dance from* The Nutcracker.

## Les Sylphides (1907)

The first version of this ballet was called *Chopin-iana*, after the composer of the music, Frédéric Chopin, and danced at the Maryinsky Theatre, St Petersburg. The Russian choreographer, Mikhail Fokine, used piano pieces by Chopin. This early version was performed mostly in Polish costumes, to honour Chopin's country. However, in a waltz, danced by Pavlova with Mikhail Obukhov, Pavlova wore a long white dress. Then costumes were changed, and all the dancers wore romantic tutus.

This second version, from 1909, was renamed *Les Sylphides* by Diaghilev. It has become immensely popular, with various arrangements of Chopin waltzes, a prelude, a nocturne and a mazurka, many of which may be familiar to you.

*Les Sylphides* has no story. It is in a romantic

Below: *For many people* Les Sylphides *is the most beautiful ballet to watch.*

Opposite: *In* Les Sylphides *dancers wear long graceful dresses.*

mood, and shows a male poet dancing with ghostly sylphs, in the setting of a ruined monastery, often among trees. The attraction is in the beautiful dancing style, with the girls in their long white ballet skirts and rosebud hairbands. Groupings of dancers in the *corps de ballet* are in lovely patterns. Smooth technique and careful line with the other dancers is needed by every performer.

The dances are not brilliant, but create a dream-like atmosphere.

Left: *Tamara Karsavina as the first Firebird with Adolf Bolm.*

## *L'Oiseau de Feu, The Firebird* (1910)

*The Firebird* music was the first that Stravinsky composed for a ballet. Diaghilev brought together many talents in this production. The young choreographer, Fokine, used the complicated rhythm of the music to express new ideas in dancing. Artists such as the painter, Bakst, were engaged to design costumes and sets. Tamara Karsavina, Fokine and his wife, Vera Fokina, as well as the dancer and teacher, Cecchetti, took part in a dazzling new ballet, for Paris.

The Russian fairy story is of Prince Ivan, who captures the Firebird. She gives him a feather, with which he can call her in time of danger, and he lets her go. Ivan falls in love with Tsarevna, and, with the help of the Firebird, delivers her from imprisonment by a wicked magician. Their wedding procession triumphantly ends the ballet.

Opposite: *A set for a 1926 production of* The Firebird *by Gontcharowa*

Below: *Rudolf Nureyev and Nadia Nerina in* Petrushka, *when the puppets come to life.*

## *Petrushka* (1911)

This ballet gave Nijinsky, a Russian dancer and choreographer, one of his greatest dramatic roles with Diaghilev's company. Stravinsky's exciting music has been made into orchestral suites, often performed in concerts today.

At a St Petersburg fair, a magician puts on show three puppets: Petrushka, who is a clown, a Ballerina and a Moor. The magician brings them all to life. Petrushka loves the Ballerina, but she prefers the Moor, who eventually kills Petrushka. The crowd is very alarmed, but the magician shows them that the puppet's body is only sawdust and wood. As he drags the broken puppet away, there is a terrible shriek, and the ghost of Petrushka appears, to curse his master.

Nureyev has danced Petrushka, acting the pathetic character by brilliant dancing.

## L'Après-midi d'un Faune,
### The Afternoon of a Faun (1912)

This was the first ballet Nijinsky choreographed for Diaghilev, and it was performed at the Paris Opéra with music by Debussy.

It was a strange composition, with the choreography not strictly tied to the music. The dancers moved in a flat-footed way, turning themselves sideways in profile, and turning their legs and feet in, not out, as in classical ballet. Nijinsky copied ancient Greek figures as seen on urns.

It is a one-act ballet and is really just an episode. A faun is playing his flute on a summer afternoon. He meets some nymphs on their way to bathe, and dances with a favourite before she leaves, dropping her scarf.

In 1953, the American choreographer, Jerome Robbins, made a modern version with two dancers meeting in a ballet studio.

Left: *A dancer from L'Opéra de Paris, dancing the role of the faun. His dancing can create a mood and be almost hypnotic.*

Opposite: The Rite of Spring, *here performed by the Royal Ballet, no longer causes a sensation, but it does create an exciting atmosphere with the mounting tension in the music.*

### Le Sacré du Printemps,
### The Rite of Spring (1913)

This ballet caused an uproar at its first performance, because the audience found Stravinsky's
music so strange and harsh. Some people objected
loudly. The dancers could then hardly hear the
music, and Nijinsky had to call out the beats for
them.

Nijinsky's choreography for Diaghilev in this
Russian work was equally startling to people in
Paris. It was so unlike the other ballets which had
delighted French audiences. The story was of an
ancient ceremony to ensure fertile crops. A girl
was chosen to be sacrificed, and she had to dance
until she died. The dancing was primitive and
seemed ugly, turning the ideas of elegant classical
dancing inside out. These jerky movements influenced the development of modern ballet and free
movement. Nijinsky's version of the ballet no
longer exists, but Massine and more recently
MacMillan have made versions.

## La Boutique Fantasque,
## The Fantastic Toyshop (1919)

Diaghilev first presented this ballet with his company in London. Leonide Massine, who was the choreographer, worked with Diaghilev for six years, having been trained at the Moscow Ballet School. The music is by Rossini.

The ballet takes place at night, when the dolls in the fantastic toyshop come to life. Two toy can-can dancers have been sold to different customers, and the plot is to prevent their separation.

Massine made many small character parts in the ballet for dancers to act as well as dance. The parts include the Snob, the Shopkeeper's Assistant, a naughty American boy and a wealthy Russian merchant. Massine was the male can-can dancer himself. The climax of Rossini's music is the famous leg-kicking can-can dance.

Opposite: *A scene from a Royal Ballet production of* La Boutique Fantasque.

Above: *Characteristic Spanish poses in* The Three-Cornered Hat.

## *Le Tricorne,*
## *The Three-Cornered Hat* (1919)

De Falla's music for this ballet is also well known in its own right. Massine made use of Spanish dances he had seen when touring Spain with Diaghilev in the 1914–1918 war. The ballet was presented in London, and Diaghilev engaged the Spanish painter, Picasso, to paint the scenery, again bringing together great talents. Tamara Karsavina and the Polish dancer, Woizikowski, joined with Massine in its first performance.

The story tells of a miller, whose beautiful wife is chased by an elderly official. The Miller becomes jealous, but with his wife outwits the rival.

## *Romeo and Juliet* (1938)

Shakespeare's play has inspired many ballets,
from the end of the 18th century onwards.
Tchaikovsky's fantasy overture, *Romeo and Juliet*,
has been used for a one-act version. Ashton composed a three-act ballet with Prokofiev's music in
1955. But the one you are most likely to see is a
three-act ballet to Prokofiev's music, choreographed by MacMillan for the Royal Ballet, in
1965. It is a splendid score, worth hearing on
record before you see the ballet.

In this story of doomed young lovers, the
dancers must be able to act, to tell the story of how
Romeo and Juliet, in spite of their love, are
separated by an ancient family quarrel, and then by
death. The Montague and Capulet families only
agree to stop quarrelling at their children's tombs.

## *Appalachian Spring* (1944)

This is a modern dance work, choreographed by
the American, Martha Graham. She used the
music of Aaron Copland, which is often played as
an orchestral piece. Merce Cunningham, an American dancer and choreographer born in 1919,
created a leading part in the ballet.

*Appalachian Spring* tells of an American couple
who have just married, and are setting up their first
home in a wilderness. They are living at a time
when people first tried to make homes in that wild
region, which was a challenge.

35

## *Cinderella* (1948)

There were six or more earlier versions of this fairytale made into ballets, but the best known one today is choreographed by Ashton, and is danced to Prokofiev's music. Ashton remembered a miniature version by the Ballet Rambert that he had seen in his youth, and from this, he built up his portrait of the two ugly sisters. They are danced by men wearing extraordinary make-up and wigs, just like pantomime dames, bullying the poor Cinderella, until the Prince rescues her.

Ashton used to dance as the meek sister and Robert Helpmann as the fierce one. Cinderella was danced by Margot Fonteyn.

*Frederick Ashton and Robert Helpmann as the ugly sisters with Margot Fonteyn as Cinderella.*

*A dramatic moment in a Ballet Rambert production of* the modern ballet, Pierrot Lunaire.

## *Pierrot Lunaire* (1962)

Here is a dramatic, modern ballet, set to the music of Schoenberg. First presented in America, it was danced by its choreographer, Glen Tetley. Since then, it has been performed by the Royal Danish Ballet and the Ballet Rambert, in England. For this production, Christopher Bruce took the leading role. The music includes speech-song, half spoken, half sung, as well as music played on a small group of instruments.

There is no exact story. The ballet shows a black clown and a white clown and a fickle, changeable woman, forever trapped in movement on and around a scaffold climbing frame.

*Pierrot Lunaire* has been filmed for television.

### The Dream (1964)

This delightful ballet has also been filmed for television. It is based on Shakespeare's play, *A Midsummer Night's Dream*. Ashton, the choreographer, used Mendelssohn's music arranged by John Lanchbery. Anthony Dowell was the first Oberon, with Antoinette Sibley as Titania. It is not often that male dancers perform on point, but Alexander Grant, as Bottom the weaver, did so for comic effect.

Oberon, the Fairy King, and Titania, the Queen, quarrel about a changeling child, and there are four human lovers who are squabbling too. Puck, Oberon's servant, enchants and confuses the four lovers. Some play-acting country people are drawn into the story, and, to tease Titania, Oberon has her bewitched. She falls in love with Bottom, one of the actors, who is wearing an ass's head put there by Puck. But the story ends happily, and all the lovers find their true partners.

*Anthony Dowell and Jennifer Penney in Royal Ballet's* The Dream.

*Titania (Antoinette Sibley) is captivated by Bottom wearing an ass's head.*

## *Tales of Beatrix Potter* (1970)

Based on the children's animal stories by the English writer Beatrix Potter, this is a film ballet. Ashton was the choreographer, and took part himself, as Mrs Tiggywinkle, a hedgehog. The music is by John Lanchbery.

The animal characters wear marvellous masks, moulded of plastic, and covered with fur or feathers. The mice hold up their long tails as they pose. Jeremy Fisher, the frog, leaps high in his smart waistcoat. Peter Rabbit, Jemima Puddleduck, Pigling Bland, Squirrel Nutkin and many others dance their way through the stories.

Above: *Merle Park and Desmond Kelly are leading dancers in this scene from the Royal Ballet's* Elite Syncopations.

Opposite: *A portrait from the ballet,* Ancient Voices of Children, *made by Christopher Bruce for the Ballet Rambert.*

## *Élite Syncopations* (1974)

This ballet is really a series of dances, as if at a dance hall, with a costumed band playing at the back of the stage. The dancers are in carnival costumes, and many of their dances are comic, or at least mocking in style. The music is called Ragtime, and there are pieces by Scott Joplin and other composers.

MacMillan choreographed the dances for the Royal Ballet, who recorded them as a television film in 1975.

### *Ancient Voices of Children* (1975)

This contrasting ballet was choreographed by Christopher Bruce for the Ballet Rambert. It has also been filmed for television. It is a modern one-act ballet for seven dancers, set to a song-cycle, with poems by Lorca. The music is by George Crumb, a modern American composer.

The ballet shows the games and quarrels of children, loving and disliking each other, in dance and mime. The ragged children have cloaks which they use as wrappers or as toys, or babies to cradle. The dancers crouch and bend and move in ways which may be unlike any other dances you have seen.

# Famous dancers

Once you have seen a ballet, you will realize that it is much more than a special kind of dancing. Ballet is a blend of several entertainments. There is the music, which is the basis for the dancing. There are the costumes and scenery, which add to the attractiveness for an audience, and there is the dancing itself. There are many styles of dancing, from dancing on point (on the tips of the toes), to writhing on the stage. It may be quick or lively movement inspired by the music, or slow pacing. There is endless variety and ballet dancers have to be able to adapt.

Left: *Two dancers from the French Ballet Theatre Contemporain demonstrating a dramatic lift in modern dance style.*

Opposite top: *Vergie Perman and Wayne Sleep in a scene from* Elite Syncopations *set to Ragtime music.*

Opposite centre: *Jennifer Penney and Mark Silver in* Swan Lake.

Opposite bottom. *The Czardas, a national Hungarian dance, performed in Act III of* Swan Lake *by the Royal Ballet.*

Ballets do not always tell a story. They may be just dancing, when the entertainment comes in watching the dancers make patterns with their bodies and seeing how they make actions beautiful. Ballets may express moods or feelings, or they may tell a story in dancing, with the characters acted by dancers.

Throughout its history, ballet has had leaders, who have introduced new styles and ideas. Some have concentrated on improving technique, to make dancers jump higher, turn more quickly, balance more easily. Some have turned back to natural movement from set steps. Some have made rules. Others have broken them.

New ideas help to keep ballet alive. Here are some of the important people in the history of ballet who have helped to make ballet what it is today.

## Louis XIV of France (1638–1715)

Classical ballet as it is known today started with court ballets. These were really pageants, parades and displays of court dances. In those days, the dancers' clothes were heavy so their movements were stately, and they used brilliant footwork. Correct ways of bowing and curtseying were practised at length by courtiers. The dances were made up of complicated patterns, performed facing the king or his queen.

Louis XIV founded the first Académie Royale de Danse (Royal Academy of Dancing), in 1661, for training dancers. The first members included his queen, dancing masters and nobles. Louis took

*Full costume for a musician playing the lute in a ballet with music by Jean Baptiste Lully, composer to the king from 1661.*

*Louis XIV of France, dressed in a costume as the Sun, for a ballet at his court, from a drawing by Stefano della Bella.*

dancing lessons every day with his ballet master, Pierre Beauchamp, and he frequently had a leading part in court entertainments and ballets.

Beauchamp introduced the turnout, by which the dancers' feet are trained to be as nearly as possible at a right angle from a forward-facing line. He also gave names to the five positions of the feet (see page 96). These are still the basis of classical ballet training today. Every movement of the dancer begins and ends with the feet in a definite position, and the arms have their matching movements. Today, ballet steps and movements still have the original French names. They are used and understood all over the dancing world. Beauchamp became ballet master at the Académie in 1671.

Jean Baptiste Lully was composer to the king from 1661. He composed over 30 ballets, music for plays and works for the Paris Opéra too.

## La Sallé (1707–1756)

Marie Sallé was the daughter of an acrobat, a member of a troupe of travelling actors. She had

*La Sallé was an 18th-century dancer who was loved and admired for her performances and especially for the dances she created herself.*

*This famous portrait of La Camargo was painted by Lancret. It shows the lightness and grace for which she was admired wherever she danced.*

dancing lessons in Paris and, at the age of nine, first appeared with her brother for 100 performances at a theatre in London. She became a favourite dancer at the French court, dancing at Paris, Versailles and Fontainebleau. La Sallé danced interludes (short dances in the intervals) in the operas of Handel, who was a friend. He composed his only ballet, *Terpsicore*, for her. Sometimes she choreographed her own dances.

Her talents were for grace and skilful miming. La Sallé created a sensation in the ballet *Pygmalion* when she wore her hair loose, and a simple muslin Greek tunic and sandals instead of a heavy costume and heeled slippers. La Sallé took the heels off her slippers, and, so that her technical feats could be seen more clearly, she daringly shortened her ballet skirts, to reveal her ankles.

## La Camargo (1710–1770)

Marie Anne de Cupis de Camargo was born in Brussels. Her father was a dancing master, who took her to Paris for dancing classes at the age of 10. There her wonderful gift for dancing became known when she was still a child. In 1727, her rivalry with La Sallé began. La Camargo's dancing was different to La Sallé's, and was much admired for its lightness and technical brilliance. Sometimes she delighted the audience by dancing solos made up on the spot. She was the first female dancer to manage steps like the *entrechat quatre*, a beating of the legs and crossing and recrossing of the feet during a high jump.

## Auguste Vestris (1760–1842)

Auguste Vestris was born into a dancing family, and became the most popular male dancer in the Europe of his time. His long career as a superb performer and teacher helped to advance ballet technique. He was taught by his father, an Italian choreographer and teacher, who was one of the first to give up the common practice of wearing masks in performances. The nickname, *le Dieu de la Danse* (the God of the Dance), was given first to his father and then to Auguste.

He first danced in pubiic at the age of 12, and was immediately recognized as having great talent. When he danced in London with his father, during 1781, parliament interrupted its sessions, so that members could go and see the Vestris's dazzling performances.

Auguste Vestris's brilliance was in his elevation, his ability to jump high. His father boasted that it was only out of pity for his friends that his son touched the ground when dancing! His turning was considered to be almost miraculous, as he seemed able to do, on one leg, what dancers before him could hardly manage on two.

He became conceited and was a difficult little man, but he passed on his technical knowledge, in teaching the Danish dancer August Bournonville, who went on to become a famous dancer, choreographer and director.

Another famous pupil was Marie Taglioni, with whom the tireless Vestris danced a stately minuet at the Paris Opéra when he was 75 years old.

*A cartoon drawing of Auguste Vestris. He enjoyed a long career, becoming popular all over Europe and was well known for his high jumps.*

## Marie Taglioni (1804–1884)

Marie Taglioni was born in Stockholm, Sweden, and studied dancing with her Italian father in Vienna and Paris. Her dancing started the romantic style of ballet. She had new soft, light dresses, in which she seemed 'like a dancing flower'. She always appeared serene and happy, and she seemed to soar when she jumped and almost to float in the

49

air. Her father said that he had never heard her land on the stage, and would disown her if he did.

She was the first dancer to perfect dancing on point. Her silk ballet shoes were only strengthened by darning on the toes, and she needed a new pair for every act of a ballet. Today's dancers have shoes

which are stiffened along the sole and the instep. There is also a block of papier-mâché in the toe of the shoe, to help balance. Her feet had to be strengthened by hard work, to support the weight of her body, and so did her ankles and back, but Taglioni showed no strain.

Her most famous role was as *La Sylphide*. She travelled triumphantly through Europe, and was very popular in Russia, influencing ballet there with her poetic style.

### Fanny Elssler (1810–1884)

Fanny Elsslcr was an Austrian and became a rival of Taglioni. Her dancing style was more dramatic and brilliant, with quick, neat footwork. One critic said that she flashed, while Taglioni flew. Fanny introduced steps from Spain into her dancing, and then later, dances from Poland and Hungary.

She was the first romantic ballerina to visit America, in 1840, and had a very successful tour, from coast to coast.

Opposite: *In this famous picture, posed in 1845, Marie Taglioni is standing with Carlotta Grisi, Lucille Grahn and Fanny Cerrito around her.*

Right: *Fanny Elssler and Jules Perrot dancing a Spanish dance called the* Castilliana Bolero.

*These drawings of Isadora Duncan give some idea of the free movement which she brought to her dancing.*

## Isadora Duncan (1878–1927)

Isadora came from America and brought her own style of dancing to Europe. She thought that traditional, classical ballet was unnatural. She took her ideas from the natural movement of trees and waves, and developed free dance, responding to the music as she felt. She chose music that was not specially written for dancing, such as pieces by Brahms, Chopin, Wagner, Beethoven and Liszt, deciding that only the greatest music would be good enough for her dancing.

To keep her dances simple, Isadora wore Greek tunics, and danced with bare legs and feet, quite unlike a normal ballet costume. When she visited

London, she was inspired by Greek sculptures in the British Museum. Sometimes she explained her ideas to her audiences. She wanted all movements to be natural, coming from simple walking, running, skipping, standing and jumping, not changed by pointed toes or turned out legs.

Trying to spread these ideas, she founded a school for 40 children near Berlin in Germany. The school was moved to Paris, and then to New York in the great war of 1914–1918. Isadora struggled to support it with dancing tours until 1919.

In 1921, she was invited to found a school in Russia, where she had been admired by many people since her first visit in 1904. But by 1924, she was poverty stricken and left Russia. She then tried to remake a career in Nice, France, writing her account of her life, supported by admirers, but often criticized. She adopted six daughters, nicknamed 'the Isadorables', who carried on her work into modern dancing.

**Anna Pavlova** (1881–1931)
Anna Pavlova was born near Leningrad, Russia, then called St Petersburg. Her first introduction to ballet was as a Christmas treat, when she saw a performance of *The Sleeping Beauty*, and immediately decided to become a ballerina. She was a poor child, but received a chance of general education and ballet training at the Imperial Ballet School.

Although she looked frail, from the age of 10, when she entered school as a boarder, Anna

Left: *Anna Pavlova dancing with Laurent Novikoff, a partner with whom she toured for many years.*

Below: *This portrays Pavlova in her most famous dance,* The Dying Swan. *The costume's glittering tutu was renewed frequently, and real feathers were used to imitate wings. Her audiences were disappointed if she did not include this dance in her performances, and Pavlova danced it hundreds of times, after the first performance in about 1907.*

developed into a brilliant dancer. She was soon promoted to the first rank of dancer, prima ballerina, and with other dancers began to take tours away from Russia. As well as classical ballet, she danced in many styles, Mexican, Indian and Spanish, studying national dances wherever she went.

She soon became extremely popular with audiences. They flocked to see her, especially in her most famous role, *The Dying Swan*, to Saint-Saëns's music.

Pavlova left Russia in 1914. In 1912, she had bought a house in England – Ivy House, Hampstead – part of which is now opened to the public as a museum on Saturday afternoons. This was her base for the rest of her life, for tours in Great Britain and all over the world. Even before the days of air travel she managed to visit 49 countries, with her own company of dancers. Anna was a pioneer, taking ballet to places where it had never been seen before, and winning new audiences.

## Tamara Karsavina (1885–1978)
Karsavina was the daughter of a dancer at the Maryinsky Theatre, St Petersburg. She was trained at the Imperial Ballet School, and became a member of the Maryinsky Company, staying with them until she left Russia after the revolution of 1917, and settled in London with her English husband, Henry Bruce.

Karsavina is remembered and loved for her great warmth and intelligence. She wrote an account of

Right: *Tamara Karsavina, one of the most famous dancers in Diaghilev's company.*

Opposite: *Nijinsky in* Schéhérazade, *a ballet set to Rimsky-Korsakov's music.*

Opposite inset: *Vaslav Nijinsky dancing with Tamara Karsavina in* The Spectre of the Rose.

her early years in Russia called *Theatre Street*, and also books on ballet technique.

When the Russian producer, Diaghilev, formed his company, Karsavina joined him on his early tours and created new roles in several ballets including *Carnival*, *Petrushka* and *Firebird*. In his first season in Paris in 1909, when Karsavina and Nijinsky were overwhelmingly popular, Diaghilev called them his 'children'.

## Vaslav Nijinsky (1888–1950)
Nijinsky was also trained at the Imperial Ballet School, where he was noted for his ability to jump high and appear to hover in the air. This astonished the French audiences in Paris, who had not seen such male dancers. They idolized him in *The Spectre of the Rose*, when he leapt through a window to appear to a dreaming girl, danced by Karsavina.

56

Encouraged by Diaghilev, Nijinsky also became a choreographer. He imitated Greek pictures in *L'Après Midi d'un Faune* (*The Afternoon of a Faun*). His *Sacré du Printemps* (*Rite of Spring*) had strange dance movements which had never been seen in ballet before, and were a foretaste of modern dance. Nijinsky's last performance was in 1919. A serious mental breakdown prevented him from completing work on ballet notation, which is the writing down of ballet.

## Martha Graham (1894–    )

Martha Graham is the founder of modern dance in America. She has been a dancer, teacher, choreographer and director of her own company. She founded the Martha Graham School of Contemporary Dance in 1927, then gathered a company from her pupils to perform in America. Later, she toured in Europe and Asia. The London Contemporary Dance Theatre, founded in 1967, and the Tel Aviv Batsheva Dance Company keep close contact with her and her methods.

The Martha Graham dance dramas use the whole body to express a feeling or mood. Unlike classical ballet, she let her dancers show the effort of what they did. Sometimes she stressed an unfolding movement from the centre of the body, not using traditional steps at all. As in Eastern dancing, her pupils were taught to shift and slide their feet, or to curl their bare toes.

Floor work is used to teach this technique. Instead of holding on to a bar for balance, the

*This picture shows Martha Graham's dramatic acting in* one of her last performances, in Phaedra.

dancer uses the support of the floor, working on the back, and sitting in various positions, with the arms, legs and head moving together. Then the dancers do exercises standing up, and finally they try various travelling steps across the studio, springing, jumping and prancing. Special falls are also taught.

Martha Graham has composed more than 150 works, in many styles, some with speech as well as music.

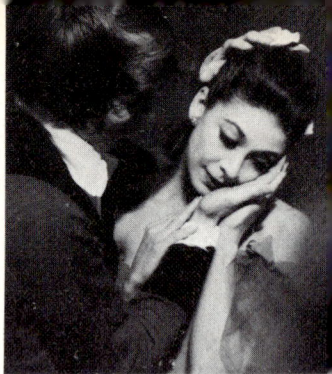

Above: *Margot Fonteyn with Rudolf Nureyev in* Marguerite and Armand.

Below: *Margot Fonteyn dancing with Michael Somes in* Horoscope, *an early ballet choreographed by Ashton.*

Above: *A very beautiful portrait of the young Margot Fonteyn as Giselle, overcome by madness.*

## Margot Fonteyn (1919–    )

Margot Fonteyn's first dancing role was as a snowflake in *The Nutcracker*, in 1934. She went on to become the star of the Royal Ballet, in London. She has had a long career, and danced beautiful farewells at the age of 60, for her friends in the ballet world at Covent Garden, London. She then made a television series, with an accompanying book, to try to explain *The Magic of Dance*, as it had enriched her life.

It is not for being a brilliant technical dancer that Margot Fonteyn has been admired for so long, with so many partners, all over the world. She is modest, and works well in a company. Her dancing reveals beauty of line and elegance, especially in her performances in *Swan Lake* and *Sleeping Beauty*. She seems naturally to dance beautifully.

This quality has been captured and interpreted in the many ballets which have been made for her by the choreographer, Frederick Ashton. His works have become the foundation of a British style of ballet. As early as 1936, he made *Apparitions* for her. A famous dance made for her with Nureyev was *Marguerite and Armand*.

As well as travelling to dance as a guest artist with many companies abroad, Margot Fonteyn has for many years been president of the Royal Academy of Dancing in London. An earlier vice-president, Karsavina, coached Fonteyn in roles which she had performed, such as *Giselle* and the *Firebird*. This made a direct link with the tradition and style of the Imperial Russian Ballet.

## Rudolf Nureyev (1938–   )

Like Pavlova, Nureyev, also a Russian, knew he wanted to dance as soon as he saw a ballet. He felt sure he had been born to dance, and was fascinated by the ability of ballet dancers to appear to be able to balance on air. By the age of eight, he was certain that he could not live without becoming part of life in the theatre, which he found so exciting. And he could not bear to be without music, to which he listened for hours on end.

At first, his parents did not encourage him to dance, so he tried local folk dancing, joining in children's troupes, and picking up what ballet teaching he could, locally. When he had auditions,

Opposite: *Margot Fonteyn with Rudolf Nureyev in a scene from* Paradise Lost.

Above: *Rudolf Nureyev dancing with Patricia Ruanne in* The Sleeping Beauty.

Right: *Rudolf Nureyev making a spectacular leap in* Les Rendezvous.

his dancing talent was noticed, and he was offered schooling at Moscow and Leningrad. He went to the Kirov School in Leningrad, and became a member of its company for three years, after what was a late start.

In 1961, Nureyev visited Paris with the company, and was enormously successful in *The Sleeping Beauty*. He then decided to leave Russia, to find more opportunities for his talent.

Margot Fonteyn invited him to dance with her, and so a popular partnership began. Nureyev has great energy, strong technique, and almost hypnotizes audiences with his strong personality.

He has danced nearly 100 roles, not only classical, but new, modern works too. He has also used his knowledge of Russian performance to produce earlier Russian masterpieces.

# Some more dancers to see today

As dancers travel, make exchanges and visits, you will be able to see those who are well established and try to pick out the new leaders of ballet.

**Merle Park**, a dancer from Zimbabwe, joined the Royal Ballet in 1954, and became a soloist in 1958. She has often danced with Nureyev, and created many roles. **Margaret Barbieri** came to the Sadlers Wells Company in 1956, from South Africa.

Below: *Lynn Seymour with Wayne Eagling in* The Invitation, *choreographed by MacMillan.*

Opposite: *Anthony Dowell and Antoinette Sibley in* Thais *choreographed by Ashton.*

**Antoinette Sibley** joined the Royal Ballet School in 1956, and enjoyed a very successful partnership with **Anthony Dowell**, who also trained there. Following a year with Covent Garden Opera Ballet, Dowell joined the Royal Ballet in 1962. After a period in America, he returned to England. **Lynn Seymour** was born in Canada and from the Royal Ballet School entered the Company in 1957. **Wayne Eagling** also came from Canada to the Royal Ballet School and joined the Company in 1969.

Above: *Lynn Seymour dancing in the title role in* Anastasia *for the Royal Ballet.*

**Wayne Sleep**, who was born in Plymouth, went into the Royal Ballet from its School in 1966, and in the '70s was creating new roles. In 1979, he choreographed a new jazz ballet for television, *Adam's Rib*.

Look out too for **Marguerite Porter**, a young star in the Royal Ballet, and **Elaine McDonald**, who has been with Scottish Ballet since 1969. **Maina Gielgud**, a versatile dancer, has produced some interesting productions, showing dance being created. **Marcia Haydée**, who was born in Brazil, made her name in the Stuttgart Ballet, and has been a guest artist in England and America.

**Patricia Ruanne** and **Eva Evdokimova** can be seen with the Festival Ballet. Evdokimova was born in Switzerland. She has a Canadian mother and Bulgarian father. She has danced with the Royal Danish Ballet, at the Deutsch Oper in Berlin and with the Kirov Ballet in Leningrad. **Mikhail**

Above: *Eva Evdokimova,
who has danced with many
companies.*

Right: *Mikhail Baryshnikov
dancing with the New York
City Ballet.*

Opposite: *Maina Gielgud
dancing with Béjart's
company, Ballet of the
Twentieth Century.*

**Baryshnikov** was also with the Kirov Ballet,
which he joined as a soloist in 1966. He now lives in
America, but often appears as a guest artist in other
companies.

These dancers and countless others, some of
whom are mentioned elsewhere in this book, move
from company to company.

# Teaching and making ballet

In the early days of ballet, it was taught entirely by a teacher demonstrating dances for the pupil to copy. It is not surprising that most of the best teachers start life as dancers. They then know exactly how to overcome problems, how to develop strength in the pupil, when to bully, when to encourage. Dancing masters used to give the beat by counting out loud, and playing on miniature violins, called kits.

A good teacher watches all the time to see where weaknesses lie. One pupil may need her back strengthening with special exercises. Another pupil may have a bad habit of hunching his shoulders.

A good pupil has to be willing to accept harsh criticism, and to work at a movement countless times to get it right. Some of the fiercest teachers, who have been known to tap the legs and feet of pupils, with a pointing cane, have been most admired, because they drew out from the pupils work of which they did not believe themselves capable. It is as if the teacher says: 'You can, because I say so,' and the dancers find that they can balance a second longer, or bend their backs a millimetre further.

Round the studio walls there will often be mirrors. In these, the dancers can look at their positions and correct them as necessary. A good teacher will set such high standards, that the pupils are never satisfied. Not only will the dancers accept correction as good for them, and useful, they will also learn to criticize their own dancing. They will know what to work at in class and rehearsal, and how to improve their performances when no one is there to shout instructions at them.

Right: *Dame Ninette de Valois teaching students at the Royal Ballet School which she founded.*

Below: *Senior ballet students working at the barre in a class at the Royal Ballet School. Notice the mirrors on the studio walls.*

Dancers also teach each other, by watching in classes and performances, and giving advice. A Russian dancer, Preobrajenskaya, warned the young Karsavina: 'Now young beauty, step off! Fire away! Control your arms if you don't want a partner minus a few teeth.'

*Frederick Ashton demonstrating steps he has created. Having prepared his choreography, he then shows dancers exactly what he wants them to do.*

Each teacher will have an individual method. Some indeed do shout. Others hardly raise their voices, but persuade, and demonstrate what they want. For music, teachers usually will have a patient pianist pounding out rhythms on the piano, as dancers' bodies are trained into obedience.

The earlier ballets were taught by retired dancers, who remembered the steps and the mime that went with them. When ballets were revived, the dancers for whom parts were originally written were sought out, to bring old parts back to life. Pavel Guerdt used to choose dances from his knowledge of old ballets suitable for the talents of his pupils. When Pavlova and Karsavina were at the Imperial Ballet School for instance, he would choose suitable dances for Pavlova's romantic grace, and Karsavina's skill in interpreting roles. Karsavina wrote:

'The most interesting part of his lesson began when the necessary routine of exercises had been got through. He then worked the steps into short consecutive dances. Often he reconstructed the parts of old ballets long gone from the stage. . . . Great dancers of the past lived again . . . .'

This passing on of ballets means that a dancer's life is a continuous process of learning, teaching and keeping up traditions.

It would be hard to exaggerate the importance to ballet of the Russian **Sergei Diaghilev** (1872–1929). Yet, he was not a dancer, nor a teacher, nor a choreographer.

Diaghilev grew up in a family devoted to music,

Below: *Picasso's design for a Chinaman's costume, for Diaghilev's* Parade.

Above: *A portrait of Sergei Diaghilev, painted by his friend, Léon Bakst.*

and he studied composition for a while. He also studied law. Then he began to take a great interest in art, and, while working for the Director of the Imperial Theatre, began to mount exhibitions of Russian painting. With his friend, the writer and painter, Benois, and the artist, Bakst, he founded a journal called *The World of Art*.

In 1906, Diaghilev took an exhibition of two centuries of Russian painting to Paris. This he followed with five concerts of Russian music, in

1907. Then in 1908 he presented his production of Musorgsky's opera, *Boris Godunov*. By 1909, encouraged by the interest of Benois and Bakst, Diaghilev had become involved with ballet. He admired the new young choreographer, Fokine, who was creating ballets less artificial than the huge spectacles of the Imperial Court. And at the Maryinsky Theatre he found a galaxy of rising stars: Nijinsky, Pavlova, Karsavina, Bolm and many others.

Diaghilev took a group of Imperial dancers to perform for a season in their holidays. The lively dancing of the men thrilled Paris, as until then, men had meekly supported ballerinas, and taken a turn to show off their abilities. But Nijinsky seemed to leap up and pause high in the air. The Russian ballerinas were worshipped too, for their floating beauty.

Diaghilev built up a company of his own. Dancers left Russia to join him, and he attracted others of many nationalities in the 20-year history of his company. His genius was in finding talents, cultivating them, then moulding them together, to make a complete artistic production.

It was not only the dancing that captivated the audiences. Diaghilev engaged Bakst and Picasso to do the scenery and costumes of his ballets. The appearance of each production with such artists was exciting. In the same way, Diaghilev asked new composers to write scores for him, works which are now admired as concert pieces as well. He provided opportunities for Stravinsky, Ravel, Satie,

Poulenc, Milhaud and Prokofiev.

Most of all, he created choreographers, by suggesting ideas, discussing experiments, and giving people chances undreamt of before. First there was Fokine, then Nijinsky, and his sister, Nijinska, and Massine.

Above: *A design for a costume in* The Nutcracker *by Benois.*

Left: *A design for a set in* Schéhérazade, *painted by Bakst for Diaghilev's ballet. The colours are brilliant, and the audiences loved them.*

Not only did Diaghilev create and revive ballets for 20 years, but he started new life and ideas in ballet, which spread all over the world. Many dancers who proudly had 'danced with Diaghilev', went on to start schools and new ballet companies in their own countries.

# Famous teachers

**August Bournonville** (1805–1879)

Bournonville's life in ballet began when he entered the Royal Danish Ballet School, Copenhagen, at the age of 12. He studied in Paris with Vestris, danced with Taglioni, had short spells as ballet master in Vienna and Stockholm. Back in Denmark, he was a soloist till 1848, but also became a choreographer, teacher and ballet master. He com-

posed more than 50 ballets, and arranged *La Sylphide*. One of his many works still performed all over the world is *Napoli*.

## Marius Petipa (1818–1910)

Petipa was a French dancer, who visited Brussels and America with his father's company, then toured in Spain, learning national dances there.

In 1847, he went to the Imperial Theatre, St Petersburg, as a principal dancer. When Petipa was made chief ballet master in 1869, he ruled and shaped Russian classical ballet into what we see today. During his long reign up to 1903, he choreographed more than 60 full-length ballets. Some of them were given giant productions, to delight the Tsar of Russia's court, but he also composed wonderful solos and *pas de deux* (duets), as in *The Sleeping Beauty* and *La Bayadère*, which are still tests of dancers' excellence today.

Opposite: *Flemming Flindt as James and Lucette Aldous as La Sylphide in a production by the Ballet Rambert of* La Sylphide.

Right: *A drawing of the famous teacher and choreographer, Marius Petipa.*

**Marie Rambert** (1888– )

She was born in Poland, and went to Paris to study medicine, but became interested in dancing and taught eurhythmics at Dalcroze's school. It was a system of translating heard sound into movements. When Diaghilev and Nijinsky visited Dalcroze, he recommended that Marie Rambert should help them with the movement in *The Rite of Spring*, with its strange rhythms.

Influenced by Karsavina, Rambert studied classical ballet herself in Diaghilev's company. Then she married, went to London, and had lessons with Cecchetti. She soon began creating her own ballets, with such new young pupils as Frederick Ashton.

This group, which she formed in 1930 as the Marie Rambert Dancers, became the Ballet Club, then the Ballet Rambert. Its base was at the Mercury Theatre, Notting Hill Gate, London. It was the first English ballet company, and still exists today.

## Ninette de Valois (1898–   )

She was born in Ireland and started dancing as a child, then went to dance with Diaghilev from 1923 to 1925. Then she came back to London, and in 1926 founded her own school. This became the nucleus of the Vic-Wells Ballet, later the Sadlers Wells Theatre Ballet, and then the Royal Ballet.

Not only did Ninette de Valois dance, but she was the choreographer of *The Rake's Progress*, *Checkmate* and other ballets. However, it is as the founder of the Royal Ballet Company and its junior and senior schools, that she will be remembered. Ninette de Valois also founded the National Ballet of Turkey, and helped with the planning of ballet companies in Canada and Iran. This spreading of ideas is typical of ballet teaching.

Opposite: *Dame Marie Rambert, who founded the oldest English ballet company.*

Right: *Dame Ninette de Valois. She retired as director of the Royal Ballet in 1963, to concentrate on the Ballet School.*

# Famous choreographers

Choreographers are the people who work out the steps of a ballet. Teachers of ballet often do some choreography, and choreographers turn into teachers when they are creating new ballets. They come to the studio and work out with the dancers what is possible, and how their ideas look when performed. Some have everything planned out, while others improvise with the help of dancers' suggestions.

Right: *George Balanchine demonstrating his choreography.*
Below: *Roland Petit with Fonteyn and Nureyev.*

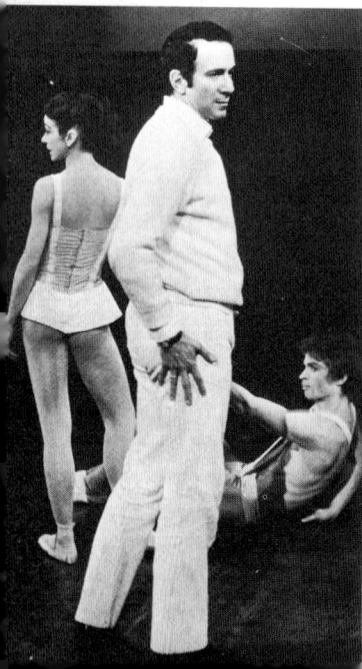

Opposite: *A scene from* The Concert, *a ballet choreographed by Jerome Robbins.*

### George Balanchine (1904– )

Balanchine has shaped a company in America called the New York City Ballet, using his early Russian training in ballet and music. He started learning the piano at five, and has always based his choreography on musical knowledge, which includes working with the composer, Stravinsky, for more than 50 years.

### Jerome Robbins (1918– )

Robbins is an American who has taught a new kind of ballet. His work spills over into choreographing the dances in musicals such as *West Side Story*, a modern version of the story of *Romeo and Juliet*.

### Roland Petit (1924– )

He is a choreographer and a dramatic actor, who has passed on that knowledge in ballets and revues in France, and in films in America. His wife, Jeanmaire, has danced in many ballets for him in Paris and Marseilles. He has also toured in London, Milan, Hamburg and Toronto.

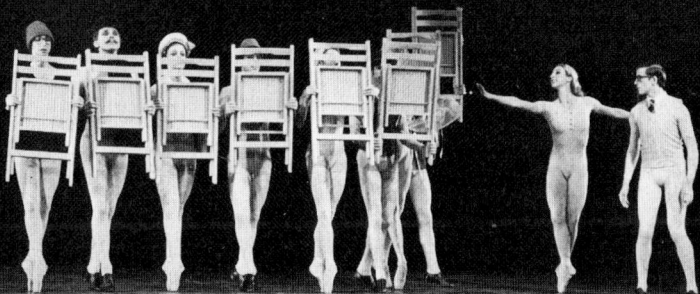

Above: *Kenneth MacMillan with the cast of* Solitaire.

Left: *Frederick Ashton with members of a ballet cast.*

Below: *A scene from* Homage to Chopin, *choreographed by David Bintley to music by Andrzej Panufnik and created for the Royal Ballet.*

**Glen Tetley** (1926– )
His works have introduced modern as well as classical styles to dancers. He started his work in America, then was director of the Stuttgart Ballet in Germany for two years, from 1974 to 1976.

**Frederick Ashton** (1904– )
In England, Ashton has created many ballets and so influenced generations of dancers.

**Kenneth MacMillan** (1929– )
He was born in Scotland, and has created new ballets, such as *Anastasia* and *Manon* since he returned to England from working in West Berlin, from 1966 to 1969.

**David Bintley** (1958– )
A very promising young choreographer, he has already created four ballets for the Royal Ballet Company, where he trained from the age of 16. Two of his ballets, *Homage to Chopin* and *Adieu*, are set to specially composed pieces by the Polish composer, Andrzej Panufnik.

Bintley feels that a person cannot be taught to be a choreographer, but is born as one, and that the best training is to have the use of a studio, a willing group of dancers and time and space to learn. Bintley had to find out, for instance, whether the 'amazing leaps' he had worked out in his head for a group of male dancers, were actually possible to do. He keeps a notebook of ideas, and finds that they come mostly from pictures, films and music.

# Modern dance

Modern dance has really been a succession of experiments, and has succeeded best when one person has pushed through his or her own ideas, however odd at first they seemed. Such a pioneer was Ruth St Denis, (1877–1968). In 1915, she and her husband, Ted Shawn, founded the Denishawn School and Company in America which taught oriental and primitive as well as modern dance.

Today, some experimental ballets do not have an orchestra playing the music but have a few musicians on the stage in sight of the audience. Others have music on tape. Electronic music is sometimes used and no music is now considered unsuitable for ballet. Choreographers are stretching dancing to the limits of what human bodies can achieve. There are no rules for the modern choreographer. He tries to create something new, which, if it is not beautiful, may be striking and exciting to an audience.

When traditional music is used, it will, obviously, have a great effect on the choreographer's ideas, as he develops them, in his head, or works them out with dancers in the studio. Ashton has said that when he is planning a ballet, he plays the music in question over and over again, and nothing else, until his brain is saturated with it.

Just as Stravinsky's music was specially commissioned for ballets, so composers today are sometimes given similar opportunities.

Twyla Tharp, born in 1942, an American dancer and choreographer, first worked out her dances without any musical accompaniment at all. With her company she would dance in gyms, art galleries or out of doors. Then, in 1971, she tried using pieces of music composed by the jazz pianist, Jelly Roll Morton, called *Eight Jelly Rolls*. Her work then became more popular. She was the first American choreographer to create a work for Mikhail Baryshnikov. This was *Push Come to Shove* with a mixture of music from Franz Joseph

Haydn's *82nd Symphony* and Joseph Lamb's *Bohemia Rag*, of 1919.

Experiments in modern ballet often bring the dancers close to gymnastics, as they are sometimes asked to do athletic contortions. To reveal the action of the bodies, dancers may wear simple body stockings, so that nothing hides their movements. Siobhan Davies, a leading dancer and choreographer with the London Contemporary Dance Theatre, admits that it can be 'quite a struggle' to do such athletic work. Sometimes even she is stiff, and she is often disappointed when she does not succeed in doing just what she wants to do. But she does not stop trying to express herself and her feelings to her audiences, and she feels that they are responding.

Below: *A scene from the ballet* Adieu *performed by Merle Park and David Wall.*

Opposite: *Graham Fletcher in* Adieu *choreographed by David Bintley for the Royal Ballet.*

# Recording ballet

There have been many attempts to write down the movements of ballet. *Labanotation*, invented in 1928, is one method which was introduced by Rudolf von Laban, a teacher and dancer who staged works for large 'movement choirs'. Modern dance companies frequently use this method.

For classical ballet, Rudolph and Joan Benesh formulated their own system of notation in 1947. It has been adopted by many companies all over the world. Dancers are now expected to be able to read a ballet score with ease. Benesh notation is based on

|  |  |
|---|---|
| Top of head | |
| Top of shoulders | |
| Waist | |
| Knees | |
| Floor | |

**▬**   Hand or foot is level with the body

**▮**   Hand or foot is in front of the body

**●**   Hand or foot is behind the body

**✘**   Bending

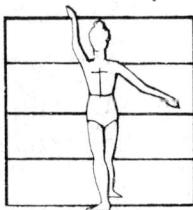
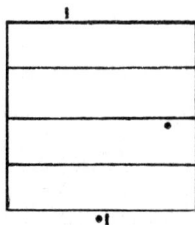

a brilliant idea, using the five line stave or set of lines which records music. The top of the dancer's head is at the top line, the shoulders at the second line, the waist at the third, the knees at the fourth and the feet standing on the fifth.

A human figure is placed in a square. Marks outline the positions of the hands and feet. Once these are known, the reader knows what the rest of the body is doing. It is a sort of shorthand. Movements are marked by curved lines, bends by crosses.

Opposite: *Diagrams to show Benesh notation.*

Below: *Using a blackboard to teach notation.*

Another modern method of recording dancing is, of course, by filming. Many companies have made television performances of their best productions. Stars, now retired, can see how they used to dance, while students following on, can see what high standards they can aim to reach. Feature films also have recorded ballet so that vast audiences can enjoy and study it.

*The Turning Point*, the story of a ballet dancer, is an example. A long-awaited film tells the story of Nijinsky's life, with extracts from the ballets of that period brought to life from old photographs, drawings and descriptions by Kenneth MacMillan. A 23-year-old American, George de la Pena, plays Nijinsky, Carla Fracci plays Karsavina, and the veteran dancer, Anton Dolin, plays Cecchetti. In such films there is an exact, repeatable record of dancing for both students and lovers of ballet to observe.

Mikhail Baryshnikov has also been recording, for American television, a sample of the many styles of dancing that he can do, in *Baryshnikov on Broadway*. As well as the classical ballet of his original Russian training, he has danced in Jerome Robbins's *Fancy Free*, and in pieces from the Agnes de Mille choreography for *Oklahoma*, wearing a cowboy hat, a top hat and a cloth cap. As director of the American Ballet Theatre he may conduct more experiments, no doubt presenting any dance he thinks worthwhile.

Opposite: *One of the many styles of dancing is shown in this scene from the film* Funny Girl.

# Different styles of dancing

Some ordinary schools have taken dancing into their timetables, as well as music and drama, because it is a way in which children can express their feelings. They can communicate by means of their dancing in a way which is unlike speaking or acting.

You have the chance of enjoying all kinds of dancing, learning to be more poised, to interpret music as you feel it. You may try out several kinds of dancing before you find the right one for you: ballet or modern dancing, folk or tap. You may have stiff legs and sore muscles until you are used to dancing. Your feet may ache at first, and you will have to follow the advice of your teachers, and perhaps have more hot baths than usual. But, if you take to dancing, in whatever style, you will find that it not only releases a lot of energy, but gives you a lot of enjoyment.

# Learning ballet

When you have watched ballet and found out something about its history, you can more clearly understand your own lessons. You can appreciate

A large group of children rehearsing. In performance it is important that everyone keeps in line with other members of the chorus, thinking of the whole scene rather than concentrating only on their own dancing.

the skill of professional dancers as they balance and turn, pose and leap. What they make look effortless, is the result of hours, then years, of hard work.

# Ballet classes

It is interesting that each dancer you admire performing with such ease on stage, has to attend a daily class. There is no such thing as a completed ballerina. The process of dancing is continuous. The body has to be kept strong and supple by exercises. Dancers come to different teachers and find fresh talents in themselves. When they learn new works they may also learn new styles from the choreographers, who may write specially for them.

Left: *This young dancer is enjoying the challenge of centre practice, dancing without the support of the barre.*

Opposite: *This girl is working on the exercises at the barre which begin each ballet class. Warming up work is done gradually so that muscles are not strained. Balance is all important.*

So every dancer will take a ballet class, which in shape will be similar to your first classes. Lessons will start at the *barre*, wooden rails placed at the side of the ballet studio. These are used to support the dancers as they limber up, bending and stretching feet and legs, keeping upright, maintaining a

good posture. Younger dancers will hold a lower *barre* so they do not have to stretch up to it.

All classical ballet movements are based on the five positions of the feet, with which each movement must begin and end. All exercises are done facing both ways, to exercise each side of the body equally, and then may be done facing the *barre*. The first exercises will be *pliés* or bends at the *barre*. These are warming up exercises to make the knees flexible, and to loosen the hip joints, so that the legs can turn out well, again based on the five positions.

Arm positions

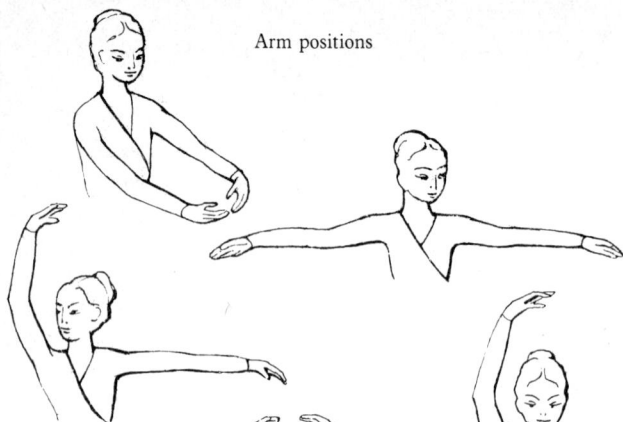

Foot positions

1.
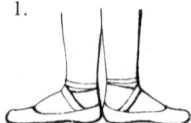

2.
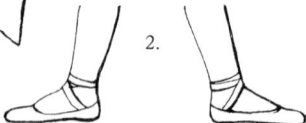

3.
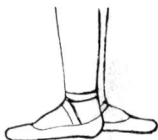

4.

5.
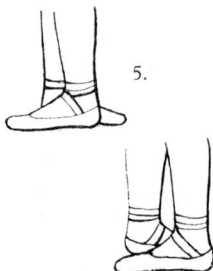

The next exercises at the *barre* may be *battements*, or beatings with the leg or foot. These exercises are for strengthening leg and foot muscles, and for exercising hip, ankle and knee joints.

The second part of the class is called centre practice. The dancers move into spaces all over the studio. Sometimes they are in lines facing the teacher. Balanced arm movements are practised. Then dancers work out steps or groups of steps, called an *enchainement*. It may be across the studio, each one in turn performing to the teacher, and receiving criticism.

The slow movements are called *adage*, and aim to develop gracefulness in the dancer. Various poses are practised, balancing the weight of the body carefully and evenly. The quicker exercises are called *allegro* and include jumps and turns in the air.

Unlike most pupils, those at ballet classes are expected to show their gratitude to the teacher before they leave the studio. Girls curtsey and boys bow at the end of class, and they also make this *révérence* to the pianist who has accompanied them, and any guest who has watched them. In a way, it is also practising for receiving applause from audiences in the future.

Opposite: *The numbers for arm positions vary from school to school, but the arms should always move smoothly from one position to another. There are five feet positions:* *1. first position; 2. second position; 3. third position; 4. two versions of fourth position with feet open or crossed; 5. two versions of fifth position.*

Left: *A teacher helping a pupil to find a more elegant pose for her arms, in a class at the Junior Royal Ballet School.*

Opposite: *Floor exercises help to make dancers' backs more flexible.*

# Ballet schools

If you show exceptional talent by the time you are nine years old, your teacher may suggest that you take an audition for a special ballet school. This means fierce competition, especially for girls. Even though it is now recognized that ballet training is as demanding as athletics, not so many boys are attracted to dancing. In fact, there are many opportunities for male dancers, and often they have a longer dancing life. Boys can start later, if they have the right, loose-limbed sort of body, and can settle to very hard training at 14. Girls usually start to specialize at 10 or 11.

A ballet school may be a boarding school, where ballet lessons are arranged for pupils in a closely packed timetable. Or dancers may attend a stage school, where they will specialize in ballet or modern or tap dancing while also taking a drama course, and ordinary school subjects. Some children manage to have ballet lessons after ordinary day school.

All children at ballet schools have to take lessons in general subjects, such as English and Maths. They need this education because if they become professional dancers they will have to be intelligent in their approach to work. Many of them will never become professional dancers, as they will grow too tall, or not be strong enough or good enough dancers to join companies. So they must be prepared to tackle other training, for other jobs.

Dancing will of course be the most important subject on the timetable, and for each pupil there will be a daily ballet class, lasting about an hour and a quarter. Girls and boys are taught separately. Girls aim for grace and strength, while hiding all the effort that it takes. Boys learn to show off their

strength in athletic leaps, controlled by disciplined muscles.

The girls probably will not start point work, until they are at least 10 years old, and have had lessons for more than two years. Then they will gradually start exercises to strengthen the feet, ankles and knees so that these can take the weight of their bodies without damage. It is a slow process. The girls with square-looking, short feet have an advantage in this, and may make quick progress in balancing on their toes in stiffened point shoes.

Not only ballet dancing, but national dancing will be taught. Students may learn folk dancing, to practise its neat footwork. They will all learn the history of ballet. Boys and girls will not work together in classes until they are about 15, when *pas de deux*, duet classes, may be attempted. Some pupils will have separate coaching classes during

*Girls working for the precision and elegance which is necessary for good tap dancing.*

the week, and the enthusiastic ones will practise by themselves to gain the steady improvement which is expected, almost demanded by teachers. By criticizing themselves in class, and by watching in the studio mirrors, pupils know whether they have danced well or not. This is essential for a performer, who must not become smug or self-satisfied, nor lazy in such a demanding art. Also there is the challenge of rivalry to win praise, and solos in displays, or small professional parts, such as in Christmas productions of *The Nutcracker*.

Ballet classes are hard work physically and mentally. Pupils have to remember instructions of lists of steps, which is good practice for memorizing roles later in their careers. Dancers need excellent memories, and must never dream in class, or they may find themselves colliding, falling, or dancing the wrong steps in the wrong direction.

*Young pupils working in the art room, making props and costumes to wear in their ballet performance.*

At some schools, pupils are given the chance to create their own ballets, in choreography classes. For this, and to study ballets, they will learn notation, the written record of ballet.

Dancing takes up most of the time for physical exercise, but pupils may also do some gym, and boys try weight-lifting. There may be swimming, football and tennis, but, as the pupils grow older, there are extra dancing classes, and most of them will be attempting examinations in general subjects by 15 or 16. Many ballet pupils take an extra interest in music, which is essential to their dancing skill, and many will fit in lessons on the piano, guitar, or another instrument.

# Further training

Those who have excelled at junior school will apply to enter the senior school, with other students from different schools and from abroad. Now the training becomes more intensive. There will be daily classes, and students will start to learn the ballets in the repertory of the company to which the school is attached. They will attend rehearsals, and, later on, be given small walk-on parts, which will get them used to theatrical life. For this, there will be classes in the use of stage make-up.

Some students may study a foreign language at this stage. It is a good idea, because there will not be enough room for all the graduate dancers in home companies, and they will need to be willing to audition, then work abroad.

Right: *Practice for a duet in a senior ballet class. The boy has to support the girl, so that her balance is perfect.*

Below: *A teacher demonstrates the step he wants practised, to a class of boys who work separately.*

Some dancers may decide to take a training course to become teachers. Another way into professional dancing is to be taken into a company and trained there, instead of in an official school. This works well with companies which specialize in a modern experimental style. A young choreographer might also be attracted to a small company, which can put on miniature new works. He can

Above: *Some last minute adjustments to beautiful ballet costumes.*

Above right: *A cast of children enjoying taking part in a ballet.*

have hopes of his work being tried out in work-shops and performances.

When students are accepted into a company, they will probably join the *corps de ballet*. From there they will hope to be noticed and given small solos, until eventually they become principal dancers.

For every member of the company, there is a hard-working routine of ballet class, rehearsal and performance. This is all the more hard work in a touring company, when they have to find time to travel as well.

Not only can a trained dancer become a teacher or a choreographer. She or he may become a notator, and record ballet, so that it can be read by

other dancers. The notator will be of great assistance to a choreographer, or to a director who is attempting a work that is new to him, or a revival of an older ballet. It is a much more exact record than the old passing down of roles, and so ballets can be preserved, at least in outline. Older dancers and teachers will then be able to concentrate on helping a dancer with the interpretation of her part, with the acting and miming, which cannot be written down.

## Mime and make-up

Acting without speaking is extremely important in ballet, where often the characters are telling a story as they dance. In the earlier works of classical ballet, such as *The Sleeping Beauty*, there were conventional signs to express 'die', 'love', 'marry'

Left: *Students learning the art of stage make up.*

Opposite: *Petrushka dancing with the Royal Ballet. You can see the effect of the completed face make up.*

Opposite inset: *The start of making up for Petrushka.*

and so on. Then, Fokine and other choreographers after him, taught the dancers to act out feelings more naturally, to express themselves as human beings, and not as unreal, dancing spirits.

Modern dance is very close to acting, and its choreographers expect dancers to be able to portray any feeling by the use of their bodies, as well as their faces.

Students are taught make-up as part of their training. It is essential to be able to make up well for appearing under stage lighting, which makes a dancer's face colourless and flat. Eyes are often emphasized for example. The dancer may have to transform her young face into that of a witch, using highlights and shadows to imitate the folds and creases in an old face.

By blending colours and practising with stage make-up, you will be able to improve your appearance for the stage. You may secretly like your looks highlighted in crimson lake, spot-lite pencil and rose blending powder, before you reach for the removing cream!

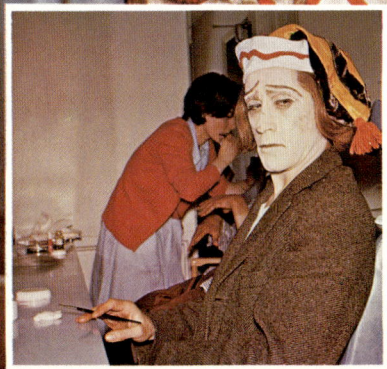

# Ballet round the world

Ballet has always been an international art. The royal courts in which it started could afford to employ dancing masters from faraway countries, for their skill and ability to bring something new to court entertainment. Royal families from different countries were often related, and could travel in a leisurely manner to other countries, to enjoy their national dancing.

From the outlines of teachers' and dancers' lives you can see that the dancing master has always been an energetic person. Most ballet masters' careers have included travel, from Russia to France, from Italy to England, from Denmark to America. The list could be long, because lively dancers travel to look for new teachers, new styles of dancing, and new audiences. Some dancers have made large fortunes doing this.

Since the days of air travel, all this movement has become faster and easier. Earlier European dancers took weeks to travel to America and Australia by sea. Now dancers can accept invitations to dance in Africa, Germany, Canada, China, all within the space of a few months, but they have to take good care of their health and stamina.

Whole companies with musicians and technical staff, costumes and scenery, travel thousands of kilometres on exchange visits. Before, it was often only leading ballerinas with their partners who were invited to visit foreign countries.

People all over the world can now see on television great dancers performing with their national companies. All the leading companies now have films of their dancing which show their special styles or excellence. People can become very knowledgeable by watching ballet on television but they do miss the excitement of attending a live performance.

Early royal patrons employed groups of dancers and sometimes the ballet masters trained their dancers in associated schools. Louis XIV founded his Académie in Paris in 1661. The Italian *Regia Accademia di Ballo* was established in Milan in 1812. The Royal Academy of Dancing opened in London in 1920.

*A young dancer waiting in the wings to make her entrance, pleased to be performing.*

*A duet from the Royal Danish Ballet's production of Bournonville's* Napoli, *with Flemming Flindt.*

# Denmark

The earliest company of dancers was the Royal Danish Ballet, founded in 1748, when the Royal Theatre was opened. There had been court ballets in the 16th and 17th centuries. Italian and French ballet masters trained the Danish dancers for many years. August Bournonville's rule from 1829 established the company, with many performances of his works. First visits abroad in the late 1940s made the Danish company known internationally. With Flemming Flindt as director from 1966 to 1978, the company has performed his experimental works as well as the classical ballets.

# Russia

The two greatest companies in Russia are the Bolshoi and the Kirov. They have their own schools, and have kept up a tradition of presenting classical ballet, with carefully trained dancers appearing at certain intervals, and leading highly

Above: *A large chorus scene from the Russian Kirov Ballet's production of* Raymonda.

Right: *Dancers from Moscow's Bolshoi Ballet taking part in* Spartacus.

regulated lives under the companies' discipline. Some dancers have wanted to perform more often, and to tackle more experimental roles, so they have left the Russian companies to become international artists. Russian companies do not tour abroad often, but, when they do, it is clear that the hard classical training still produces technically superb dancers. Smaller experimental companies and folk dancing groups are occasionally seen too.

*A chorus of Japanese dancers from the Tokyo Ballet in a scene from* Le Palais de Crystal.

# Japan

The technical mastery gained by a Russian training is much admired by teachers. The Tokyo Ballet, founded in 1964, has been helped and influenced by Russian teachers. Ballet has become very popular in Japan. There are many schools and, by 1975, there were eight companies in Tokyo.

# Great Britain

In Great Britain, national ballet was established in the 1930s, as The Sadlers Wells Ballet, under the inspired leadership of Dame Ninette de Valois. Its first journey abroad was to Paris, in 1937. During 1956, it became the Royal Ballet. It now has a junior school, a senior school and a home theatre at Covent Garden, London. A smaller group has had a varied history, trying out experimental ballets, touring throughout Great Britain, and sometimes using Sadlers Wells Theatre as a base. This is called the Sadlers Wells Royal Ballet.

Ballet for All is a little group which visits schools and small theatres to dance excerpts from the repertory of the Royal Ballet.

The Ballet Rambert, also founded in the '30s, now a small company, tours with many experimental works, at home and abroad.

Another major British company is the London Festival Ballet, which grew out of a company that Alicia Markova and Anton Dolin assembled around themselves. The first performance by the company was in 1950, and ever since then, it has always aimed to give popular performances of the classics and to welcome many guest stars.

The London Contemporary Dance Theatre was founded in 1969, and specializes in modern dance. Often, the dancers choreograph their own works

*Dancers from the London Contemporary Dance Theatre showing the striking poses that modern dancers can make.*

and take them on tour. Dancers and choreographers who have created new works include Robert Cohan, Robert North and Siobhan Davies.

Scottish Ballet took this name in 1974, following a move to Glasgow, where the company is based, and a change of title from Western Theatre Ballet. Another excellent company is the Northern Dance Theatre, serving the north west of England. There are also many small companies such as the Extemporary Dance Company.

# North America

America has been the birthplace of modern dance, and many companies carry on this tradition. Two major companies are the American Ballet Theatre and the New York City Ballet.

Arthur Mitchell, a black dancer, left the New York City Ballet in 1968 to take up teaching in Harlem, where he was born. He started a school in a garage, with the doors left open for passers-by to join in. Thirty students grew to 400 within a year. Karel Shook joined Mitchell from the Dutch National Ballet, where he had been ballet master. This company has remained black, and taken the name Dance Theatre of Harlem.

In Canada, The National Ballet was founded in 1951. It is based in Toronto, but tours around Canada and abroad. Recent tours have been in the USA, Europe and Japan. Other companies include Grands Ballets Canadiens and The Royal Winnipeg Ballet.

Below: *New York City Ballet performing* Union Jack.

Above: *Dancers from the National Ballet of Canada.*

Below: *A duet from* Allegro Brillante, *danced by the American Dance Theatre of Harlem.*

# Germany

The Stuttgart Ballet is one of the liveliest companies in Germany, and, since its first tour abroad, to the Edinburgh Festival in 1953, it has become world famous. It has its own school, and pupils have been able to board there since 1971. Since Filippo Taglioni and his daughter, Marie, visited The Stuttgart Ballet between 1824 and 1828, visitors have been welcomed, and they give new life to the works being performed. The South African, John Cranko, who became a choreographer at the Royal Ballet, went to direct the Stuttgart Ballet in 1961, and built up a marvellous troupe of dancers and a large repertory before his death in 1973.

# Italy

In Italy, there are many small touring companies, which come together for a while, then are disbanded. In the summer, many cities such as Florence and Spoleto, welcome them, and foreign touring companies, for their Festivals.

# Australia

The Australian Ballet originated as The Borovansky Ballet. Its first performance was in 1962. It now has its own school and a large repertory. There are other smaller companies of classical and modern dance, and many schools throughout the country.

Above: *Australian Marilyn Burr with Austrian Karl Musil.*

Right: *Liliana Cosi from La Scala company in Italy.*

Below: *Choreographer John Cranko with dancers.*

# Holland

The Dutch National Ballet has a high reputation for performance and choreography, but as yet no national ballet school.

# France

France, the royal cradle of ballet, gave its leading choreographer, Petipa, to Russia. During Diaghilev's time, France was a centre of ballet. Serge Lifar, who danced with Diaghilev, directed the company at the Paris Opéra from 1929 to 1945. Violette Verdi was made director in 1977. Today there are many other dance companies of all sizes.

Opposite: *Maria Koppers (Dutch National Ballet) in* Firebird.

Above: *A scene from* Le Grand Défilé *by the Paris Opéra.*

Companies are rather like families, and obviously have arguments and disagreements, as families do. The 'children' of companies grow up and move away, so the members of a company change. Guests come visiting. It is the director, his staff and the ballet masters and mistresses, who have to keep the dancers, not only in training trim, but working well together to produce good performances. They work hard to link up the music, movement, drama and beauty into an artistic spectacle for audiences to enjoy.

# More books about ballet

These are books in which you can look up more about ballet as you watch new works, or learn more dancing yourself.

*A Legend for Dancers*, the Story of Anna Pavlova: Robina Beckles Willson (Hodder & Stoughton, 1981). Even today, more than 50 years after her death, Anna Pavlova is not forgotten. She was educated at the Imperial Ballet School, in St Petersburg (Leningrad), but left Russia to become a pioneer for ballet. Using England as a base, she toured all over the world. She was an adored soloist with her own company, and took ballet where it had never been seen before.

*The Beaver Book of Ballet*: Robina Beckles Willson (Hamlyn, Beaver, 1979). This is a beginners' guide to learning ballet. It describes life in a ballet school, and gives you ideas for what you can do later with your own training. There are some useful hints on enjoying music and drama in your spare time.

*The Encyclopedia of Dance and Ballet*: Mary Clarke and David Vaughan (editors) (Pitman Publishing, 1977). This is an excellent reference book. It is well illustrated, and you can look up information about classical and modern dance.

*The Young Ballet Dancer*: Liliana Cosi (Ward Lock, 1978). This attractive book is translated from Italian and deals well with ballet technique and going on stage.

*Classics of the Royal Ballet*: Jesse Davis (Macdonald and Jane's, 1978). The following ballets are described in detail and illustrated by good photographs: *The Nutcracker*, *Swan Lake*, *La Fille Mal Gardée*, *Giselle*, *Romeo and Juliet*, and *The Sleeping Beauty*.

*A Dancer's World:* Margot Fonteyn (W H Allen, 1978). For Margot Fonteyn, 'the world of dance is a charmed place', but this does not prevent her from presenting in this book a most practical and helpful guide to young dancers. She deals with early training, examinations, life in a company and as a teacher. She also describes other kinds of dancing as well as ballet.

*Every Child's Book of Dance and Ballet*: A H Franks (editor) (Burke, 1957, revised 1972). This collection of articles includes interesting descriptions of two ballet dances, two mimed dances and two national character dances, which can be tried out with the music provided.

*Better Ballet*: Richard Glasstone (Kaye & Ward, 1977). You can find help in understanding your classical ballet lessons in this book. It describes what is learnt in class. There are photographs of dancers demonstrating steps and movements with great clarity. There is also a useful glossary of ballet terms.

*Male Dancing as a Career*: Richard Glasstone (Kaye & Ward, 1980). All the information needed by a boy considering a life of dancing is found in this book. It is the first book of its kind written for young male dancers, who can use it to find out about ballet, tap, stage, and modern dancing, or dancing purely for pleasure. Richard Glasstone teaches at the junior department of the Royal Ballet School, and gives details of further training and possible careers for boy dancers.

*Life at the Royal Ballet School*: Camilla Jessel (Methuen, 1979). Superb photographs of the daily life of pupils, working and playing at the school, give a full account of the process of becoming a dancer. It is a fresh and lively portrait of the pupils' way of life in the junior department.

*The Concise Oxford Dictionary of Ballet*: Horst Koegler (editor) (Oxford University Press, 1977). This is a reference book which is easy to consult, and gives you clear definitions of technical words, material on dancers' lives and the ballets they dance.

*Beginning Ballet, From the Classroom to the Stage*: Joan Lawson (A & C Black, 1977). This is a first book for ballet students of all ages. It includes an interesting section of instructions for making stage costumes, national costumes, and, for classical ballet, a tutu, a leotard and a crossover.

*Your First Book of Ballet*: Odon-Jérôme Lemaitre with Yvette Chauviré (Angus & Robertson, 1976). This book is particularly interesting on choreographers. It also lists ballet schools.

*The Facts about a Ballet Company*: John Percival (G Whizzard/André Deutsch, 1979). John Percival features the Sadlers Wells Royal Ballet in an interesting and detailed account of a touring company. He gives facts not often found elsewhere, about management, accompanying classes and orchestras. This is of great interest to young readers who cannot dance well enough to join a company, but want to work with ballet.

*Enjoying Ballet*: Jean Richardson (Hamlyn, Beaver, 1977). This paperback gives a lively account of ballets, with helpful advice on how to enjoy attending performances.

*A Young Person's Guide to the Ballet*: Noel Streatfeild (Warne, 1975). Here is the story of a boy and girl who start dancing at nine and learn about themselves and their talents as well as about ballet and its history.

*Ballet Guide*: Walter Terry (David & Charles, 1976). This is useful for looking up different ballets. Over 500 are described with illustrations.

# Ballet music

All these pieces have been used for ballet. Some, like Tchaikovsky's and Stravinsky's works, were specially written as ballet scores. Other pieces gave the choreographers their ideas. Try to buy or borrow recordings of these pieces or listen to them on the radio. Then, when you watch the ballets, your pleasure will be increased because you know the music. There is an enormous variety, and you may even like the music so much that you don't just sit and listen, but start dancing at home.

| Music | Composer |
|---|---|
| *Apollo* | Stravinsky |
| *Appalachian Spring* | Copland |
| *Apparitions* | Liszt |
| *Barcarolle* | Offenbach |
| *Bayadère, La* | Minkus |
| *Bolero* | Ravel |
| *Boutique Fantasque, La (The Fantastic Toyshop)* | Rossini |
| *Carnaval, Le* | Schumann |
| *Checkmate* | Bliss |
| *Cinderella* | Prokofiev |
| *Coppélia* | Delibes |
| *Cygne, Le (The Dying Swan from The Carnival of Animals)* | Saint-Saëns |
| *Dream, The* | Mendelssohn |
| *Enigma Variations, The* | Elgar |
| *Façade* | Walton |
| *Fancy Free* | Bernstein |

*Giselle*    Adam
*Hamlet*    Tchaikovsky
*Jeux d'Enfants*    Bizet
*Job*    Vaughan Williams
*Lied von der Erde, Das*
   (*Song of the Earth*)    Mahler
*Noces, Les*    Stravinsky
*Nutcracker, The*    Tchaikovsky
*Oiseau de Feu, L'* (*The Firebird*)    Stravinsky
*Orpheus*    Stravinsky
*Patineurs, Les* (*The Skaters*)    Meyerbeer
*Petrushka*    Stravinsky
*Pierrot Lunaire*    Schoenberg
*Pineapple Poll*    Sullivan
*Polovtsian Dances* (from *Prince Igor*)    Borodin
*Prelude à l'Après-midi d'un Faune*    Debussy
*Ritual Fire Dance*
   (from *Love the Magician*)    de Falla
*Rodeo*    Copland
*Romeo and Juliet*    Prokofiev
*Sacré du Printemps, Le*
   (*The Rite of Spring*)    Stravinsky
*Schéhérazade*    Rimsky-Korsakov
*Sleeping Beauty, The*    Tchaikovsky
*Spectre de la Rose, Le*
   (ballet to *Invitation à la Valse*)    Weber
*Swan Lake*    Tchaikovsky
*Sylphides, Les*    Chopin
*Symphonic Variations*    Franck
*Symphonie Fantastique*    Berlioz
*Tricorne, Le*
   (*The Three-Cornered Hat*)    de Falla

# Index